WHAT DID YOU DO IN THE WAR DADDY?

WHAT DID YOU DO IN THE WAR DADDY?

A VISUAL HISTORY OF PROPAGANDA POSTERS

INTRODUCTION BY PETER STANLEY

A selection from the Australian War Memorial

Melbourne
OXFORD UNIVERSITY PRESS
Oxford New York

OXFORD UNIVERSITY PRESS

Oxford London Glasgow New York Toronto
Delhi Bombay Calcutta Madras Karachi
Kuala Lumpur Singapore Hong Kong Tokyo
Nairobi Dar es Salaam Cape Town
Melbourne Auckland
and associates in
Beirut Berlin Ibadan Mexico City Nicosia

© the Australian War Memorial 1983
First published 1983

This book was designed and produced by
Tamerlane Pty. Limited,
14 Gladesville Road,
Hunters Hill, New South Wales 2110, Australia,
in association with The Australian War Memorial, Canberra

National Library of Australia
Cataloguing-in-Publication data:
Stanley, Peter
What did you do in the war, Daddy?
Bibliography.
ISBN 0 19 554404 8.

1.   Australian War Memorial.   2. Political posters.
3.   War.   4.   Propaganda.   I. Title.

769'.4935502

Designed by Judy Hungerford
Typeset by B&D Modgraphic, South Australia
Printed in Singapore by Kyodo-Shing Loong Printing Industries
Published by Oxford University Press, 7 Bowen Crescent, Melbourne

CONTENTS

INTRODUCTION

The British poster artist 'Fougasse' defined posters as 'anything stuck up on a wall with the object of persuading the passer-by'. To persuade the passer-by is the essential function of propaganda. By 1914 city dwellers in Europe, North America and Australia had become used to seeing posters as an everyday part of their street-scapes. Posters had acquired the fundamental elements of their design through the development of concise text and simple illustration and, on the fringes of fine art, were accepted as a serious form of visual expression. But it was as a tool of commerce and industry and not as an aspect of decorative art that posters became established. In the half century before the outbreak of the 1914-18 war, illustrators and printers produced pictorial posters to publicize, inform and advertise. It was relatively easy, therefore, for the poster industry to convert on the outbreak of war to the service of persuasion as part of the belligerent nations' war efforts.

The Great War stimulated the evolution of the propaganda poster as it did many other areas of technological change and innovation such as the development of aircraft or motor cars. The war effort annexed artists and craftsmen and the techniques and conventions they had devised, and harnessed them to the most intensive use of graphic art seen up to that time. It was probably the most extensive mobilization of printed pictorial propaganda for political purposes in history. Millions of copies of thousands of designs were produced. James Montgomery Flagg's inspired adaptation of Alfred Leete's poster [Kitchener] *wants you* alone ran to over five million copies.

Posters became 'the weapon on the wall', pervasive munitions in the battle for minds which mirrored the war in the trenches. Posters were an ideal means of delivering propaganda. By their nature they dealt in slogans and simple, quickly comprehended visual images. They were cheap to produce, easy to distribute, and already accepted as a medium of communication. Under the pressure of total war poster designers found ways of promoting and persuading which even the competition of prewar business had not required. While many designs simply employed conventional contemporary advertising techniques on themes related to the war, the more sophisticated poster artists, especially those of Germany and central Europe, were able to extend the prosaic advertising poster of peacetime into compelling, and even moving, advertisements for war.

Posters were used by governments in wartime to manage, through the use of symbols and slogans, the opinions and actions of their populations. Though respected artists were associated with poster art in both world wars the war poster is in some ways the opposite of art. Art is able to extend our conceptions of the nature and possibilities of life, but the war poster's purpose was to restrict its viewers' understanding. A successful poster was one capable of only one interpretation. Most of the posters reproduced in this book did not seek a dialogue: they imposed, imparted and impelled, but did not inquire. They sought to persuade the viewer, and then to have him or her act in ways regarded as useful by the sponsors of the poster.

The first Australian posters appeared in 1795 when George Hughes printed letterpress advertisements for plays being performed in Sydney. Until the mid-nineteenth century the majority of Australian posters comprised auction notices, official proclamations such as 'wanted' posters and playbills, mostly in letterpress form. Overseas developments in lithography were brought to Melbourne in the 1850s by a Scandinavian immigrant named Charles Troedel. In partnership with Edward Cooper, Troedel pioneered the Australian pictorial poster and by the outbreak of the 1914-18 war advertisers had festooned railway stations and public hoardings with a variety of advertisements, many of the most memorable being for beer. With the exception of the work of Harry Weston and Blamire Young no consciously artistic poster art had evolved by 1914 but the medium and its producers were to be used to the full in the propaganda campaigns which occurred in the streets of Australia during the Great War.

The posters which from the spring of 1914 appeared on blank walls all over the country fulfilled some of the conditions of effective propaganda in that they were one-sided, repetitive and consistent. For all their imperfections they represented the most insistent and bitter campaign of persuasion which Australia has ever seen.

Australian posters of the 1914-18 war were concerned above all with recruiting men for the Australian Imperial Force which from April 1915 was engaged in Gallipoli, Palestine and, above all, in France and Belgium. Recruiting campaigns were co-ordinated by the Commonwealth government and by State recruiting committees working through voluntary local bodies. Their fragmented direction, the rudimentary state of the advertising industry and the amateurism of the organizers resulted in some extremely poor examples of graphic art. Many posters were adapted or used without alteration from British and, after 1917, from United States sources. This should be borne in mind when viewing Australian posters, especially those of the early years of the war. As many ideas and designs were simply copied, many posters do not reflect Australian perceptions of the war.

In spite of this, the posters offer valuable insights into the kinds of appeals which were made to eligible young men and, more significantly, into the sentiments which the poster designers and sponsors felt were appropriate to promote. Australia had entered the war because of its ties with Britain and, although imperial connections were employed frequently, the most evident feeling emerging from a study of the posters is a distinctively nationalistic one. Not surprisingly for a nation whose 'birth' was hailed, even during the war, as having occurred on the cliffs above Anzac Cove, the 'digger' quickly became a recognizable archetype. Early in the war the uniformed heroes on posters were simply cheerful and hale young men but by 1915 the digger was instantly recognizable from his upturned hat, broad chest and firm jaw. The war poster must be credited with some part in popularizing to those at home the figure of the Great War digger.

Other peculiarly Australian images originating from before the war were pressed into service. The somewhat sentimental 'little boy from Manly', first used by The Bulletin to exemplify the Australian identity, was used as well as the more readily recognizable kangaroo. The war also assisted in the recognition and acceptance of the Australian flag, which appeared in both red and blue and was not yet as powerful a device as the Union Jack.

Sporting imagery figured strongly in posters designed in Australia. A poster printed by Troedel and Cooper seeking men for the 'Sportsmen's Thousand' depicted a soldier of the Victorian 23rd Battalion. The soldier, in a similar pose to Alfred Leete's Kitchener, points directly at the viewer and baldly addresses the eligible with the words 'Man you *are* wanted!' juxtaposing the Victoria Cross with a collection of sporting impedimenta and asking

'Which?' The caption to another poster seeking sportsmen urged them to enlist together, train together, embark together and fight together, though no specifically sportsmen's battalions were raised in Australia as they were in Britain. The masculinity of the eligible was the target for some other posters. 'It is nice in the surf', a New South Wales 'Win the War League' poster asked, 'but what about the men in the trenches?'

In some States appeals were made to men in specific country regions. As might be expected such posters were technically and psychologically less finished than products of capital city printers. A poster addressed to the men of western Queensland, for example, appeared entirely in letterpress, while a design authorized by the Rockhampton recruiting officer included a crude drawing of a digger surrounded by a rather confused border of admiring or helpless children. The text of this poster illustrates the unsophisticated approach of many Australian recruiting appeals and seems to contain more examples of characteristically Australian recruiting clichés than any other. Opening with the somewhat negative assertion that 'Some men seem to think they can live for ever!' it asked whether the eligible were 'game to take the sporting chance' which the Anzacs had taken by enlisting. Raising the unwritten law of mateship it invoked 'the spirits of your dead pals' who 'send their cooee'. Was the shirker going to let 'the greatest democratic army in the world' dwindle? Be a man!, it urged, 'Enlist today!'

As the war progressed the need for reinforcements grew greater than the willingness or ability of the population to supply them. Increasingly, Australian posters concentrated on the spectre of the extemely remote, if not fictitious, threat of a German invasion of Australia. In 1915 the Hun was portrayed as identical to the barbarians who sacked Rome in 451 AD. In 1916 a poster appeared showing Zeppelin raids and stating that 'by staying at home you are giving your approval to this kind of thing'. There was some ambiguity about whether the target of German bombs was London or Melbourne, and compared to the hysteria of 1917 and 1918 the modest euphemism of referring to air raids as 'this kind of thing' impeded the poster's value as propaganda. Harry Weston's *Would you stand by while a bushfire raged?* made the point more effectively, by linking the German menace to one of the most frightening and destructive dangers of Australian rural life. Weston's work, unlike the Zeppelin poster, met the criteria of good design, and, in leaving the viewer to make the connection between the bushfire and the object which it symbolised, anticipated Fougasse's technique of drawing the audience into the design.

The disparity between the symbols in which propaganda deals and the reality which it attempts to influence can be seen, in the Australian context, by the dominant imagery of recruiting posters of 1918. By this time the Australian Government was desperate for recruits. Conscription had twice been rejected in two bitterly contested referenda campaigns in 1916 and 1917, though Britain and New Zealand had adopted compulsion in 1916, followed by Canada in 1917.

The German invasion of Belgium in 1914 had provoked a stock of atrocity stories, some based on supposed fact, others on flagrant lies, which formed the popular impression of the Hun for the rest of the war. German 'frightfulness' was constantly invoked by Allied propaganda—Queensland women, for example, were reminded of the invasion of Belgium and asked to 'think what horrors women and children in Queensland will be subjected to, unless Germany is beaten'. The image of the spiked-helmeted Hun ravaging the country had become established in the imagination of Allied civilian populations. It was an image used, above all, by Norman Lindsay in the series of six posters which he produced for the Commonwealth's last recruiting campaign.

Lindsay's designs carried with them the impetus of four years of anti-German propaganda. His cartoons for *The Bulletin* initially portrayed Germans as bumbling figures of fun but became more threatening as the war progressed. By 1918 his Germans had become vicious brutes. The posters *Will you fight now or wait for this* and *The peril to Australia* show the fate which would befall Australia if it were conquered by Germany. *Will you fight now* . . . illustrates German soldiers executing a man cowering against a distinctively Australian corrugated iron water tank. He represents those men who would not fight the Hun in Europe and were now reaping the rewards of their cowardice. The second depicts the arrival of German soldiers in an Australian town. The noticeable feature of these two posters, and many more like them in Britain and the United States, is their use of powerful imagery which played upon the sexual attitudes of their intended audience. This is most evident in *The peril to Australia* which is captioned 'This may be *Your* Sister's Fate', and shows burly Germans hauling frightened young women away to presumed molestation and rape. In the first poster the main incident is the shooting of the man at the water tank, but the psychological impact of the poster lies in the detail at the centre in which the young woman, her dress torn open, is restrained by two Huns. The effect of this detail, to which the viewer's attention was drawn by the levelled rifles, would have been far greater than its prominence suggests. Through the use of the image of the defilement of womanhood, one of great contemporary potency, it would have attracted the viewer's attention immediately. The impact of the scene may even have forestalled the question of why the woman, who is apparently dressed in street clothes, is not wearing underclothing.

By 1918 it appears that the symbol of the Hun imposing 'Kultur' on conquered civilians had assumed a life of its own, completely divorced from the reality of the war in Europe. The Germans of Lindsay's 1918 posters with their *picklehaube* helmets are those who invaded Belgium in 1914, not the exhausted trench-fighters who were by that time retreating from machine-gun post to machine-gun post towards their own frontier.

The campaign in which the Lindsay designs were employed deserves attention, because it was the culmination of the government's imposition on the Australian people of a particular perception of the enemy and the war. Australian pictorial propaganda had come a long way from the Union Jack hoardings of 1914. The first of the six posters, usually known as ?, featured the most savage image which any nation employed during the Great War. The bestial figure, also known as 'the Ogre' or the 'German Monster', with its blood-stained hands grasping a globe, stood unmistakably for German militarism.

The poster prompted questions in Federal parliament. Mr. J. W. Leckie asked the Minister for Recruiting whether 'the placarding of the city and country towns with a horrible poster of a gorilla dripping blood over the world is likely to have a good effect in inducing eligibles to enlist . . .?' In response to a further question from Mr. F. Brennan, who sought the Minister's view on the 'repulsive pictorial incitements to bloodshed', the Minister for Recruiting replied that it was 'just possible that the poster . . . might bring home to eligibles the methods of the enemy whom we are fighting'. It undoubtedly brought the enemy's worst methods home to Australian people. The poster produced much public comment after it was secretly distributed overnight in October 1918. Lindsay's ? echoed, or possibly inspired, a similar poster in the United States.

Five other posters were intended to be released at intervals coinciding with postal notices to each eligible man but the armistice intervened and the campaign was abandoned after the fourth poster. The barbarity of the first design has tended to obscure the remaining posters of the series. As pictorial propaganda they were not successful. The second poster, *Quick*, which showed Australian troops in extremity calling for aid, was needlessly defeatist, as was *God bless dear Daddy*, a well known poster featuring a careworn woman mournfully praying with her daughter. The fourth, *Will you fight now . . .* was plainly misleading. The final two designs, *The last call* and *Fall in*, though not publicly displayed were contradictory in that the former untruthfully implied that the Allied forces were in danger of failing—an implication refuted by newspaper headlines—while *Fall in* showed a cheerful line of recruits such as had not been seen since 1915.

Lindsay's posters reflected less a planned propaganda campaign than his own obsessions. In Britain and the United States Frank Brangwyn's 1918 design *Put strength in the final blow*, which showed an Allied soldier bayonetting a German, was censured, rather ironically, for depicting needless violence. In Australia Lindsay's ? however, attracted comment rather than controversy. He justified the savagery of his work, believing that 'a country that kills the killer in man will be destroyed by any other country which has preserved the instinct to kill'. Lindsay did his best to preserve that instinct in the last months of a war in which it had been tested to the limit.

British poster propaganda of the 1914-18 war, unlike newspaper and leaflet propaganda, was distinguished by its amateurism and by what is today regarded as its naivity. Its appeals were wordy and homely, rarely achieving the effective insidiousness of Savile Lumley's *Daddy, what did you do in the Great War?*, or the vigour of L. K. W.'s *Forward to victory*, both of which appear in this book. British designers were largely unable to exploit the national or sporting identification which appeared in Australian posters. They drew instead on a variety of cultural and specifically wartime themes. The posters which they produced appear in retrospect to have less power than they exhibited at the time. The appeal of Lawson Wood's 1914 poster *A chip off the old block*, which informed its viewers that 'Your King and Country need you to maintain the honour and glory of the British Empire' appears hackneyed to an age which no longer values king, country or empire as they were once valued. As the numbers enlisted in Kitchener's new armies testified, however, the appeal of such concepts was not negligible.

British posters were largely the work of printers and lithographers. Unlike their European counterparts, very few artists besides Frank Brangwyn and Gerald Spencer Pryse produced posters. The reliance on tradesmen rather than artists, however, increased the impact of the posters among working class people, who comprised the majority of their audience. Because they were produced to the instructions of more or less graphically illiterate sponsors by printers who were experienced in commercial advertising, the posters closely resembled pre-war advertisements. The unsigned poster *The kitchen is the [key] to victory* is the product of such a system, and illustrates wartime propaganda's inheritance from civilian advertising. The poster's similarity to the advertisements which people had seen every day before the war meant that the message was communicated easily. The woman could almost have been advertising a type of kitchen range or a brand of gravy.

More consciously artistic posters, such as William Frank's national war bonds promotion featuring the Duke of Wellington, relied for their impact—which in any case was aimed at the better-off middle class—on a more educated audience. Its slogan 'Up civilians!' recalls Wellington's 'Up guards and at 'em', spoken on the field of Waterloo, a rather abstruse connection for the man in the street.

British posters drew on diverse traditions of visual dispay. The placard seeking 4000 fruit pickers in Scotland, for example, is little more than illustrated letterpress, following the leisurely conventions of Edwardian publicity. An accompanying drawing informs the viewer that the men at the front would appreciate the pickers' efforts but its meaning is obscure without careful scrutiny. The Parliamentary Recruiting Committee, the major sponsor of British poster art in the 1914-1918 war, published *The veteran's farewell* which harks back to the sententious Victorian tradition of story-pictures. It fulfilled its function in a way that would have been obvious to a society acutely conscious of class and its manifestations. By carefully including men of many styles of class-related dress—muffler and cloth cap, a bowler and suit—the artist has communicated that all classes were required to enlist. Yet, its message could have been communicated, more explicitly and concisely, as it would have been in Germany, and characterizes Britain's amateur attitude to both the war and the propaganda it inspired.

The United States did not enter the war until 1917 and her troops were only engaged in France from the summer of 1918 until the armistice in November. America's war propaganda organization, the Division of Pictorial Publicity, however, was mobilized and fully utilized within months of her involvement. It turned out thousands of designs which in the main were superior to those of Britain or Australia.

American posters were generally produced by professional artists with training in art schools or with experience in book or magazine illustration or commercial art. Some artists, such as James Montgomery Flagg or Howard Chandler Christy, whose designs featured attractive women in patriotic poses, became as well known for their poster art as for their pre-war work. As in every belligerent nation, however, a good deal of hack work was done to meet the demands of government policy. In the United States, where sympathy for the Allied cause and the desire for neutrality vied for support until the declaration of war, atrocity propaganda using the images of 1914 emerged and became a major element in the government's campaigns to mobilize public support for the war. Identical themes were used as in other Allied nations: the jackbooted, spiked-helmeted ravager of Louvain, the crucifixion of our boys and the rapists—both metaphorical and literal— of Belgium.

Although American posters varied in quality—from the meticulous illustration but stilted design of Michael Whelan's parade ground soldiers and G. R. Macaulay's crude figure for the 1917 Liberty Loan campaign, to Flagg and Christy's art—most United States designs were strongly figurative and often realistic in style. Most were simpler and better drawn than the workmanlike British and Australian designs and contained much less text. They reflected the strengths of the Madison Avenue advertising techniques which between the wars would come to dominate business in the western world.

Continental posters, a few examples of which appear in this collection, were often more justifiably described as poster art. While less mediocre work was produced by unskilled printers, the practice of holding poster competitions to coincide with war loan campaigns and other charitable appeals often resulted in poor amateur posters appearing in public. National differences are evident between French and German designs. French artists favoured drawings rather than blocks of colour. Jules Faivre's *On les aura!*, is representative of the best of French work in this style. German designers produced the most artistic of any national style. Though generally more diverse than French work their posters were more sophisticated and, of all Great War posters, are more likely to retain their appeal to the present day. German poster artists paid much more attention to the typographical elements in their designs, seeing the integration of text and illustration as of much more importance than in other national styles, and generally combined the text with single dominant images such as a flag, an eagle or a figure.

Between the two world wars an understanding of propaganda emerged as a significant part of the study of the experience of modern war. Poster art, stimulated by the impetus of war, had become a sensitive tool of commercial advertising. By the outbreak of the 1939-45 war, however, new processes had overtaken the poster as the primary means of influencing the public. Radio, sound motion pictures, newsreels and popular newspapers, had been either introduced or perfected and were to be instrumental in carrying the burden of messages which in 1914-18 had been communicated by posters. The poster therefore became an adjunct, albeit an important one, to the more important media of radio and film. At the same time, improvements in techniques and developments in the poster's use made it a more effective means of influence.

Posters of the 1939-45 war differed from those of the previous conflict in several important respects. They were generated largely by designers and copywriters who had acquired their skills in commercial advertising rather than in the printer's shop. As advertising artists were employed in teams of designers, photographers and lithographers working in response to clients' requirements they were easily co-opted into the war effort; sometimes the only alteration for an agency was that the client became the government. Their work avoided the extremes of amateurism which characterized many earlier war posters, and was more professional and prosaic. Posters of the 1939-45 war were also more realistic, more humorous and, despite the intensity of the struggle between competing ideologies, less earnest. Perhaps the major difference between the posters of the two world wars was that those of the second sought, to a far greater degree, to change the behaviour of those at whom the posters were directed. In the Great War most posters were designed largely to channel national feeling toward the war effort; in the 1939-45 war many more posters appeared which required civilians to actually do things as well as believe that their cause was just.

Britain became, with the exception of the Soviet Union, the most intensively organized of the belligerent nations. Pressure on both human and material resources called for the utmost care in their distribution and use and posters were one of the most important means by which the population was alerted to the need for economy. The purposes to which posters were put in support of Britain's war effort illustrates their increased range of uses in the second world war. Posters were used to buttress patriotism, caution security, urge greater production or reveal the nature of the enemy. Of the thousands of posters which were printed, the few selected for this book include designs carrying appeals to dig for victory, warnings to beware of spies, reminders to spend wisely, verse in honour of London transport conductresses, encouragement for factory workers and exhortations to support the fighting forces.

One of the most striking features of British posters, in contrast to their poor showing in the first world war, is their quality. Even though most of the styles employed have become obsolete, the initial appeal of many British posters can still be seen. The legacy from contemporary commercial advertising is readily apparent. This can be seen directly in the 'Squander Bug' series, which appeared in reduced form as newspaper advertisements in Britain and Australia. *Keep Mum, she's not so dumb*, for example, could almost be an advertisement for whisky or perfume. The lessons of advertising are also apparent in the combination of visual ploys used in the Army Education Scheme poster *What can you do in Civvy St.?* An obviously liberated demob suit on a street of career opportunities was directly related to the desires of thousands of British servicemen waiting to go home at the end of the war.

British posters conveyed a strong sense of the commonplace. Few dealt in the rhetoric of glory. Their tone was not that of God and Empire as in 1914-18, but was one of determination rather than bravado. The characters on the posters are ordinary people; the clippie is no Edith Cavell, the soldier smiling over extra blankets is no firm-jawed hero. In the people's war ordinary people asked their fellows for greater efforts. It may be that by rejecting the 1914-18 propaganda picture of 'the Hun' and allowing the entirely more human idea of 'Jerry' to appear, British propaganda won much more than simply the war.

As in the first world war the United States developed a range of posters in pursuit of the aims of government. American designs were much more concerned to show ideological differences between the opposing sides than were the more utilitarian British posters. From the trauma of Pearl Harbor and the early reverses in the Pacific war, United States posters concentrated on the 'war of ideas', as a US Office of War Information poster put it. These posters, for example *Stay on the job until every murdering Jap is wiped out!*, were some of the most grotesque produced by the western Allies. Some, such as John Falter's *Sacrifice for freedom* made their point by references to German sadism, though in a milder form than in 1914-18.

One of the ironies of the reaction from the excesses of the propaganda of the 1914-18 war was the general belief that 'propaganda was all lies'. This conviction led to widespread scepticism in the west at stories of the Nazi holocaust, which, had it been exploited, would have been a powerful propaganda weapon. More positive ideological posters were designed by Norman Rockwell, whose *Ours . . . to fight for* summed up the ideals of a democratic America in a realist, if not realistic, style.

Despite greater experience in commercial advertising, more abundant resources and advanced technology, American poster design, though often more economical in text and imagery, was less successful than British work. This was partly because American posters concentrated on abstractions such as *Avenge December 7* rather than telling people that coughs and sneezes spread diseases, or that careless talk cost lives. When American designers did come to grips with their audience they succeeded in producing some very effective applied art. Wesley's *'. . . because somebody talked'* appears somewhat sentimental now, with its dewy-eyed spaniel mourning its master's loss. Of the four elements in the design—the caption, the sailor's collar, the spaniel and the banner—the last is today the least noticeable. Yet the poster would have been deciphered much more readily, indeed, instantly, in 1943 because all of its viewers would have known that the banner, given to the relatives of servicemen killed in action, immediately communicated to the viewer the loss of the dog's owner. In wartime this was a symbol of enormous power for, as it appeared in the windows and on the walls of thousands of homes across the United States, it conveyed to those who saw it sadness and bereavement.

As so often happened in areas of cultural expression, Australian posters borrowed from British and American sources. Though maintaining, partly through the isolation of war, vestiges of an idiosyncratic Australian character, the posters of the 1939-45 war were much closer to overseas designs than those of the 1914-18 war had been. Reflecting the diverse requirements of the management of a complex modern war economy, the posters promoted many utilitarian themes; to eliminate absenteeism, conserve resources, increase production and maintain security. Australian images did appear—the cockatoo in Warner's poster counselling silence, or Norman Lindsay's pop-eyed Aussie in *The Austral •••••aise*—but, like references to Australia's imperial heritage and obligations, they were submerged by many more posters which could have originated in any western country at war.

Australian posters were produced by civilian commercial artists working under contract for the government and official designers working within departments and authorities. Other posters appeared under the imprint of the various cartographic and survey companies of the Australian military forces.

Many designs were inferior to overseas work. Two of the Commonwealth Coal Commission's posters, for example, *Trim that lamp!* and *Coal must be saved!* illustrate the mediocrity of posters issued in Australia. *Trim that lamp!*, apparently based in part on a panel of Norman Rockwell's *Ours . . . to fight for* appears, at first sight, to compare the obedience required of Japanese workers with the freedom of discussion of the Australian way, but it is in fact calling for greater efforts in the winning of coal. The meaning of the words 'trim that lamp!' is unclear. Quite apart from the weak visual potential of a picture of a block of coal, *Coal must be saved!* is a poor poster. It consists predominantly of text and has none of the humour of comparable British posters to soften its strident tone.

On the other hand, Australian poster artists, although making relatively little use of overseas techniques such as photo-montage and cartoons, did create competent and even attractive designs which effectively communicated their messages as well as those produced in Allied nations. *Gunner Digby*, one of a series of 'apt epitaphs' designed by the Junior Tactical School of the First Australian Army, employed an arresting and colourful illustration for a pointed jingle. The Australian Red Cross Society, which relied for its funds entirely on voluntary donation, was promoted widely by poster. A romantic Red Cross poster, effectively combining the strong statement of the red cross with the ethereal light and angelic pose of the nurse, appears in this book. The crudely-finished poster *Wipe out the shadows*, directed against industrial absentee-ism illustrates once again that the value of a poster lay in the way in which it was intended to be or was received and not on the way it appears today. *Wipe out the shadows* may be an amateur effort, but in using the readily recognizable symbol of the Japanese rising sun it conveyed its message to those who were intended to appreciate and act upon it.

Posters were used to supplement propaganda messages presented to large groups, such as those liable to buy war bonds, or to reinforce messages directed at smaller groups, such as housewives, farmers or industrial workers. Posters were not, however, always the most appropriate medium for such messages. The poster *Hi soldier!* is impeded by text of a length and style more suited to a wireless advertisement that to a poster, which usually depends on a strong visual symbol and a brief slogan to make its mark. Perhaps the poster was meant to be digested during the interminable delays which soldiers experienced in transit camps and waiting rooms.

While it would be difficult to judge the actual effect of posters at the time, judged by the criteria of successful propaganda, Australian posters as a whole were not very effective. The insistent, carefully calculated and professionally executed designs of Britain and America were rarely equalled. No repetitive slogan was promoted which was as powerful as the United States 'You are a production soldier, America's first line of defense!' and no Australian slogan attained currency as a catch-phrase as did 'Is your journey really necessary?' in Britain. On the other hand nor was the divisiveness of much Australian poster art of the 1914-18 war equalled.

The 200 posters in the Memorial's collection which appeared in opposition to Australia's involvement to the war in Vietnam represent almost the only posters of protest in the 8000 posters which make up the collection. This is significant because, being cheap and easily manufactured and distributed, posters have often been used as the ideological weapons of protest or of revolutionary groups. Posters were widely used, for example in central Europe in the 1920s, in the United States in the 1960s and 1970s, and in France in 1968. The posters included in this selection, however, and in many other anthologies, are overwhelmingly those of the powerful rather than those of the protesting.

Most of the posters produced during the two world wars were designed to influence the opinions and change the behaviour of the belligerent nations' own people rather than to demoralize the enemy. One is left with the somewhat disturbing realization that wartime poster campaigns were waged against civilian populations by their own governments. This is not always evident from the posters themselves, which often call for compliance in actions which we can see would have been in the viewers' interests. Sometimes the guard slipped, as in the notorious 'red poster' issued by the Chamberlain government early in the 1939-45 war, which ambiguously informed Britons that

Your courage
Your cheerfulness
Your resolution
Will bring *us* victory

That civilians were most often the target of official poster propaganda explains the paradox of the virulence of Australian posters during the 1914-18 war. Australia publicly proclaimed itself committed to the Empire's struggle, even to the 'last man and the last shilling'. Its government was, however, forced to extract the compliance of its people by insistent, divisive and increasingly savage propaganda which harped on a grotesquely improbable Hun threat by slurring and harassing its men and using its women as manipulative symbols. Australian propaganda of the Great War, though innocently patriotic in 1914, produced by 1918 some of the most persistent and misleading imagery of any non-totalitarian nation.

Readers of this book will be struck by the similarities between war posters of different nations. This is not simply the result of plagiarism—though designs such as Faivre's *On les aura!* and Leete's [*Kitchener*] *wants you* were borrowed and adapted. It was often the result of designers arriving at solutions to common problems because the needs of the combatant powers—to mobilize, persuade and regiment their populations in the interest of national war efforts—were similar. National, stylistic and functional differences occurred in the context of this purpose.

Posters employed a great many images to convey their messages. Personifications such as 'John Bull', 'Uncle Sam' or 'Marianne' and archetypes such as Tommy Atkins, the digger or the *poilou* appeared in 1914-18. Symbols such as flags, guns, tanks and ships or symbolic evocations of peace or victory such as nursing mothers were employed in both wars.

Even national mythology and history were conscripted, Britain using Nelson, the Duke of Wellington and St George to persuade young men to enlist. The wars themselves produced a range of images, the potency of which has diminished since 1918 and 1945. In the first world war Belgium, the *Lusitania*, Louvain and Edith Cavell were powerful words, the mere mention of which being sufficient to suggest in the popular imagination the excesses of Hun frightfulness. It is worth noticing, in discussing the manipulation of symbols, that Edith Cavell, while appearing in posters as a beautiful young woman, was in fact middle-aged and rather homely.

Social stereotypes were also used in a variety of contradictory ways. In the first world war British women were depicted as patriots prepared to tell their menfolk to 'Go', as damsels in need of protection, as good sports willing to don khaki, as frugal housewives holding the key to victory and as cheerful workers on farms or in hospitals. These symbols were directed at different sections of the population. They were called upon again in the next war in rather more sophisticated ways, with the addition, in less sexually squeamish times, of the figure of the 'easy girlfriend' who was unfairly blamed for increased rates of venereal disease.

Authors and editors of works on pictorial propaganda often speculate on the effectiveness of war posters. For historians, as for the sponsors of the posters themselves, the question is impossible to answer authoritatively. Means of ascertaining their impact are imperfect. Some information on the reaction to poster propaganda employed in the 1939-45 war can be obtained through opinion polls, Mass Observation in Britain, security agencies or the correspondence columns of newspapers. For the 1914-18 war the historian must rely on more impressionistic sources. The caption to the most famous British poster of the war, *What did you do in the Great War, Daddy?*, was parodied during the war on a Donald McGill-style picture postcard depicting a hen-pecked husband answering his son's question with 'Just as I was told, my lad—just as I was told'. This suggests that the poster succeeded as a catch-phrase, but whether it succeeded in what it set out to convey is open to question.

Fougasse considered that before a poster could persuade or impel action it must attract attention. Apparently many posters failed even to be noticed and often could not convey their messages. George Orwell found that at the outbreak of war in 1939 many Londoners could not distinguish between the 'alert' and the 'all clear' sirens, even after months of seeing air-raid precautions posters. The posters described the alert as a 'warbling' note but it transpired that few people attached any definite meaning to the word.

Because posters were used as instruments of government policy they were usually displayed with a definite end in mind. It may even be that the function of many posters was simply to be seen, to contribute to an atmosphere of involvement in the war effort. This may explain the number and variety of 'careless talk' posters, even though, in Britain, the United States and Australia the effort of producing and distributing such posters far outweighed the damage which enemy agents could have achieved. Indeed in Australia, it was known that no spies were active.

The value of these posters to students of the century of total war is considerable. They give valuable insights into the aims and methods of those who ran the war efforts and influenced the lives of millions of people, from the faceless virtuosi of national propaganda policy to the amateur patriots of the State recruiting campaigns.

A collection of posters, along with newspapers, newsreels and popular songs, enables us to experience the environment in which the citizen-at-war lived. The pressure on eligible Australian men and their families during the Great War is felt with the clarity of direct experience from a perusal of these posters. The philosophy of Nazism, to which millions of Germans were exposed, can be found in the captions of posters of the Nazi era; 'We may perish but Germany must live!', 'Without blood, no life; without sacrifice, no liberty!' and 'The Fuhrer is always right'. In some respects the reality of wartime life can be recaptured with more success from the ephemera of war than from the narrative of more 'significant' events.

We should become acutely sensitive to the intentions and methods of such historical evidence. Even though the Great War is still part of the memory of some living Australians, its poster propaganda, which offers such rich insights into the values and attitudes of both government and people, deals in images, concepts and slogans which represent radically different values from those of our own. The slogans of 'God, King and Empire' or the images of diggers, Huns and symbolic virgins follow conventions which may not be familiar or accessible to the scholars of the present day. If we dismiss them as 'mere propaganda', or as indications of the gullibility of our grandparents, we will neglect an important link with the minds and feelings of humanity at war.

Peter Stanley

THE POSTERS

AUSTRALIA   1914-1918   76 x 50 cm
Artist: Norman Lindsay
From a series of Norman Lindsay's recruiting poster/pamphlets. It
depicts the conquest of Australian towns and women by German troops

AUSTRALIA   1914-1918   97 x 64 cm
Artist unknown
A good example of an Australian poster copied without alteration from
the Parliamentary Recruiting Committee original. The figure is
completely dressed and equipped as a British soldier

(PAGE 22)
AUSTRALIA   1914-1918   76 x 50 cm
Artist: Harry J. Weston
The immediacy of war versus the casual image of sport. The soldier is
contrasted with a young man, lounging in a deck-chair, smoking and
drinking — his sports equipment nearby

(PAGE 23)
AUSTRALIA   1914-1918   91 x 59 cm
Artist unknown
Issued by the Government Printer in Sydney, this recruitment poster
depicts airships bombing a town, with an inset of a woman and
children being injured by an enemy bomb blast

AUSTRALIA   1914-1918   76 x 50 cm
Artist: Norman Lindsay
Depicts soldiers fighting desperately, and pleading for assistance. Issued
in 1918 by the Commonwealth Government

ENLIST
BY
STAYING
AT
HOME
YOU ARE GIVING YOUR APPROVAL
TO THIS KIND OF THING
W. A. GULLICK.
GOVT. PRINTER,
SYDNEY.

TO THE MEN OF AND CENTRAL

Some men seem to think they can live for ever!

And are not game to take the sporting chance the Anzac took when they sacrificed themselves for you!

Are you going to tarnish the fame of Australia by hesitating and shirking your job?

Are you content to hide yourself behind the blood of men and the sorrow of women?

Remember the unwritten law!

"This is the law of Australia
As sure and as certain as fate,
Take your share of your troubles going
And never go back on your mate."

ROCKHAMPTON QUEENSLAND.

Your mates are clamouring for reinforcements. The spirits of your dead pals send their cooee too "We have given all, are you going to betray us?"

Are you going to let the greatest democratic army in the world dwindle day by day.

HESITATE NO LONGER!
JOIN THE COLOURS!
SHOULDER A GUN!
BE A MAN!
ENLIST TO-DAY!

[R.O., ROCKHAMPTON.]

AUSTRALIA   1914-1918   44 x 29 cm
Artist: B. E. Pike
A regional war poster aimed at the men of Rockhampton and central Queensland. The appeal is to patriotism and virility: 'Join the colours! Shoulder a gun! Be a man!'

AUSTRALIAN IMPERIAL FORCES
SPECIAL APPEAL
TO
WESTERN MEN

250 WESTERN MEN WANTED 250

All Men entering Camp from Districts near Western Line at same time (about end of June) may be trained and sent away together.

Applications to Enlist should be made immediately to the nearest Recruiting Office.

COME ALONG, LADS!
and show what the Western Men can do.

AUSTRALIA   1914-1918   62 x 48 cm
Artist unknown
A special appeal to 'western men' issued by the Queensland Recruiting Committee

(PAGE 26)
AUSTRALIA   1914-1918   100 x 74 cm
Artist: H. M. Burton
A soldier stands astride the Dardanelles with his hands cupped to his mouth. A call for enlisters: 'Coo-ee- Won't you come?'

(PAGE 27)
AUSTRALIA   1914-1918   100 x 72 cm
Artist unknown
A soldier makes a direct appeal for sportsmen to enlist. Note the Victoria Cross and sports equipment counterposed

AUSTRALIA   1914-1918   76 x 50 cm
Artist unknown
A poster from the Queensland Recruiting Committee featuring maps at
the war-fronts and a soldier pointing the way to war

A CALL FROM THE DARDANELLES

"Coo—ee—
Won't _YOU_
come?"

GULF OF SARO

GALLIPOLI

SEA OF
MARMORA

ENLIST NOW

Issued by Authority of THE DEFENCE DEPARTMENT OF THE COMMONWEALTH. ——— S.T. LEIGH & CO. LTD. LITHOGRAPHIC PRINTERS, SYDNEY.

WHICH?

MAN
YOU ARE WANTED!

IN THE SPORTSMEN'S 1000

TROEDEL-COOPER PTY LTD

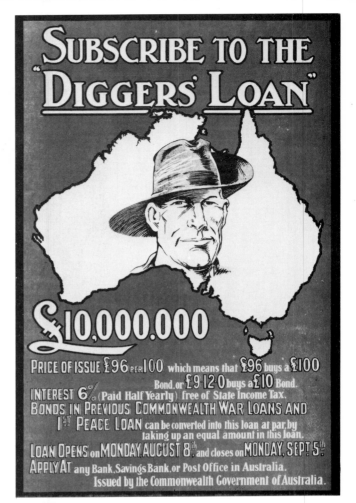

AUSTRALIA   1914-1918   89 x 57 cm
Artist unknown
A Hun is a Hun is a Hun . . . whether in 451 A.D. or 1915. The
option is clearly spelled out: Join the Australian Imperial Force in order
to protect women and children from a barbaric enemy

AUSTRALIA   1914-1918   76 x 51 cm
Artist unknown
Perhaps the most obvious symbols of a country at war: a 'Digger'
superimposed on a map of Australia. Poster issued by the
Commonwealth Government

(RIGHT)
AUSTRALIA   1914-1918   75 x 50 cm
Artist unknown
An appeal to the strong woman behind each willing soldier —
issued by the Queensland Recruiting Committee

AUSTRALIA   1914-1918   119 x 78 cm
Artist: *Norman Lindsay*
A soldier trumpets for assistance from the front line while civilians listen
in the distance

AUSTRALIA   *1914-1918*   *76 x 50 cm*
Artist unknown
A recruitment poster featuring a proud kangaroo before a group of
charging soldiers

(RIGHT)
AUSTRALIA   *1914-1918*   *76 x 50 cm*
Artist: Harry J. Weston
A poster from the New South Wales Recruiting Committee featuring a
blazing bushfire as a symbol of the German threat to Australia

Would you stand by while a bushfire raged?

GET BUSY, and drive the Germans back!

WIN THE WAR LEAGUE. I SERVE

Issued by the N.S.W. Recruiting Committee.

IT IS NICE IN THE SURF

BUT

What about THE MEN IN THE TRENCHES

GO AND HELP

WIN THE WAR LEAGUE
I SERVE

AUSTRALIA   1914-1918   76 x 50 cm
Artist: Souter
A man who should be at war is shown enjoying himself in the surf.
- *Issued by the 'Win the War' League*

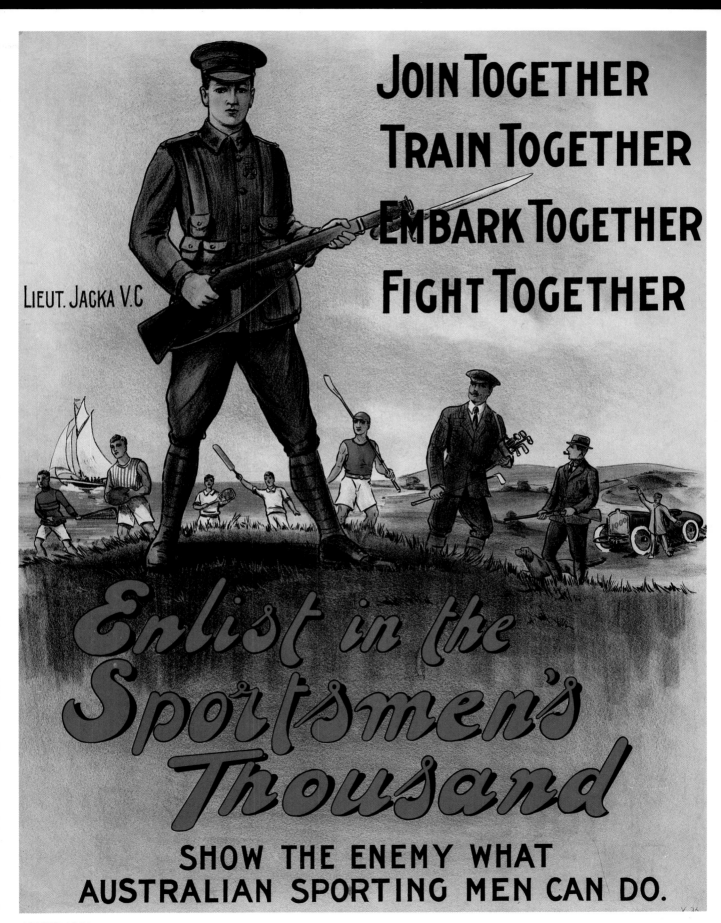

AUSTRALIA   1914-1918   119 X 78 CM
Artist unknown
Lt. Albert Jacka V.C. is featured 'showing the enemy what Australian
sporting men can do'

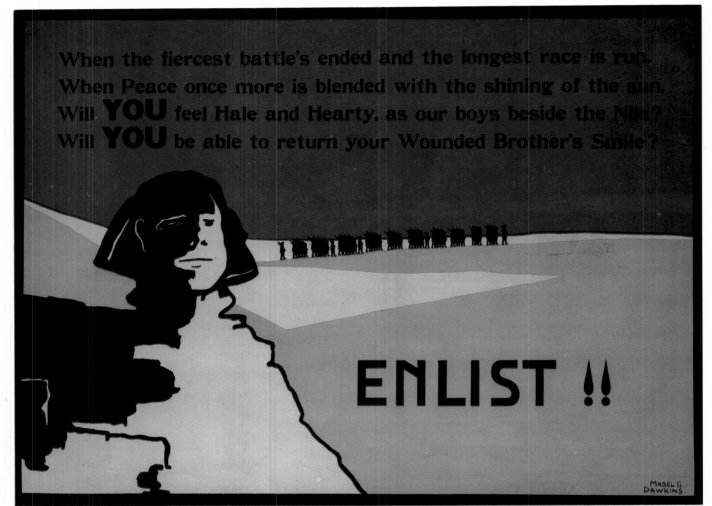

AUSTRALIA   *1914-1918*   *68 x 91 cm*
Artist: Mabel G. Dawkins
Dominated by the figure of the Sphinx, this poster shows soldiers
marching in the desert. Issued by the State War Council in Adelaide

(RIGHT)
AUSTRALIA   *1914-1918*   *99 x 72 cm*
Artist: J. S. Watkins
A particularly powerful poster, issued by the Queensland Recruiting
Committee. A woman raises her fists in anger. Two children lie dead at
her feet, her hair is in disarray and a breast naked

(PAGE 36)
AUSTRALIA   *1914-1918*   *50 x 34 cm*
Artist: Norman Lindsay
Features a wounded soldier amongst the dead, bugling for assistance
from a trench on the Western Front

(PAGE 37)
AUSTRALIA   *1914-1918*   *50 x 38 cm*
Artist: Norman Lindsay
A German ogre with blood-drenched hands grasps greedily at the
world

The Last Call

ISSUED BY THE GOVERNMENT OF THE COMMONWEALTH OF AUSTRALIA.

W. E. SMITH, LTD., SYDNEY

ISSUED BY THE GOVERNMENT OF THE COMMONWEALTH OF AUSTRALIA.

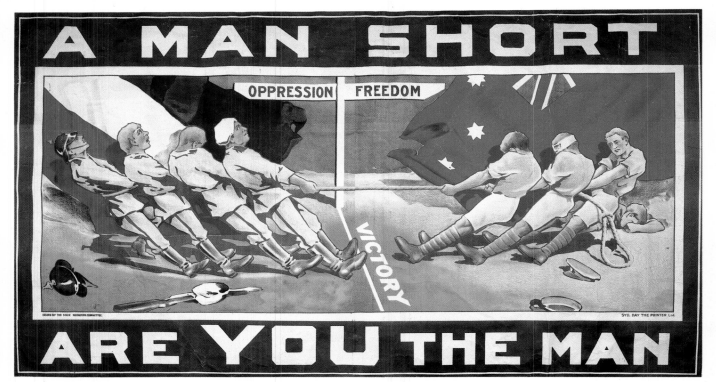

AUSTRALIA   *1914-1918*   *112 x 200 cm*
Artist unknown
The clear division between the oppression of Germany and Australian
freedom, graphically portrayed as a tug-of-war. Note that the
Australians are out-numbered!

Will you fight now or wait for This

ISSUED BY THE GOVERNMENT OF THE COMMONWEALTH OF AUSTRALIA.

W. E. SMITH LTD., SYDNEY

AUSTRALIA   1914-1918   93 x 76 cm
Artist: Norman Lindsay
An Australian recruiting poster depicting German soldiers savaging a
grazier, his wife and children

THE QUESTION.

WHICH ROAD SHALL WE TAKE?

GREAT BRITAIN   1914-1918   39 x 26 cm
Artist: H. M. Raven
Depicts a signpost pointing two ways: one to German peace where dark clouds loom, the other to British peace where the sun shines cheerfully over attractive countryside

NATIONAL SERVICE
WOMEN'S LAND ARMY

APPLY FOR ENROLMENT FORMS AT YOUR NEAREST POST OFFICE OR EMPLOYMENT EXCHANGE

GREAT BRITAIN   1914-1918   76 x 51 cm
Artist unknown
The war effort continues on the land. A country girl fills a trough with hay for a horse and foal

(RIGHT)
GREAT BRITAIN   1914-1918   76 x 50 cm
Artist unknown
A Scottish soldier points to an appealing rural scene. Thatched cottages, colourful gardens and hedgerows . . . threatened by the enemy

(PAGE 42)
GREAT BRITAIN   1914-1918   76 x 51 cm
Artist unknown
A woman in W.R.A.F. uniform points to the air-force symbol in an appeal for recruits

(PAGE 43)
GREAT BRITAIN   1914-1918   74 x 50 cm
Artist unknown
An enlistment poster issued in Dublin by the Organization of Recruiting in Ireland. The figure on the right has a shamrock in his hat-band

British Women! — the Royal Air Force needs your help

as **CLERKS,**
WAITRESSES
COOKS, experienced
MOTOR CYCLISTS
& in many other capacities.
Full particulars from the nearest
EMPLOYMENT EXCHANGE
ENROL AT ONCE IN THE

W·R·A·F.

WOMEN'S ROYAL AIR
FORCE

GREAT BRITAIN   1914-1918   76 x 50 cm
Artist unknown
A recruitment poster depicting a young girl, dressed in uniform,
beckoning new recruits for the Queen Mary's Army Auxiliary Corps

GREAT BRITAIN   1914-1918   76 x 51 cm
Artist unknown
The key to victory is thrift . . . a woman stands in front of her oven, a
steaming pan in her hands. Poster issued by the Ministry of Food

(RIGHT)
GREAT BRITAIN   1914-1918   76 x 50 cm
Artist: Savile Lumley
The emotional impact of family pride. Young children ask their father
about his military prowess

(PAGE 46)
GREAT BRITAIN   1914-1918   75 x 51 cm
Artist: Lawson Wood
An elderly veteran wishes a soldier well as he prepares to board a train
for the Front. Poster issued by the Parliamentary Recruiting Committee
in London, 1914

(PAGE 47)
GREAT BRITAIN   1914-1918   51 x 74 cm
Artist: Frank Dadd
A poster issued in 1914 by the Parliamentary Recruiting Committee,
London, depicting a Chelsea pensioner shaking the hand of a young
soldier. Enlistees can be seen in the background

Daddy, what did _YOU_ do in the Great War?

YOUR KING & COUNTRY NEED YOU

A CHIP OF THE OLD BLOCK.

TO MAINTAIN THE HONOUR AND GLORY OF THE BRITISH EMPIRE

GREAT BRITAIN   *1914-1918   77 x 51 cm*
Artist: Herbert Pizer
An appeal for fruit-pickers to collect crops before spoiling. Nourishment
for soldiers and sailors engaged in the war effort

(PAGE 50)
GREAT BRITAIN   *1914-1918   51 x 38 cm*
Artist: William J. Franks
A British war poster featuring the Duke of Wellington, Arthur
Wellesley. An appeal for civilians to purchase war bonds and savings
certificates

(PAGE 51)
GREAT BRITAIN   *1914-1918   74 x 51 cm*
Artist: E. V. Kealy
A mother, daughter and son embrace as they watch soldiers marching
bravely to war

(PAGE 52)
AUSTRALIA   *1914-1918   74 x 50 cm*
Artist unknown
The emotional bond between mother and son used for powerful effect to
promote the sale of war bond loans. The tranquil background contrasts
strongly with war hostilities — a reminder of the hope for eventual peace

(RIGHT)
GREAT BRITAIN   *1914-1918   76 x 51 cm*
Artist unknown
Mythology adapted to war. A war poster showing St George slaying
the dragon. Issued by the Parliamentary Recruiting Committee, London

(PAGE 53)
AUSTRALIA   *1914-1918   102 x 72 cm*
Artist unknown
An enthusiastic crowd welcomes a warship back to port, but the appeal
is for peace bonds as well as patriotism

WOMEN OF BRITAIN
SAY –
"GO!"
Published by the PARLIAMENTARY RECRUITING COMMITTEE, London. Poster No. 75
Printed by HILL, SIFFKEN & Co. (L.P.A. Ltd.), Grafton Works, London, N.

WOMEN!
HELP AUSTRALIA'S SONS
WIN THE WAR
AUSTRALIA
BUY
WAR LOAN BONDS

Men Wanted for the Army

(ABOVE)
UNITED STATES OF AMERICA   1914-1918   96 x 72 cm
Artist: Michael P. Whelan
A fine poster depicting soldiers in uniform — a bugle-call for recruits

(RIGHT)
UNITED STATES OF AMERICA   1914-1918   96 x 72 cm
Artist: H. R. Hopps
A remarkable American war poster depicting a girl being carried away
by a gorilla wearing a German helmet and brandishing a club

THE SHIPS ARE COMING

UNITED STATES SHIPPING BOARD EMERGENCY FLEET CORPORATION

ISSUED BY
PUBLICATIONS
SECTION
EMERGENCY
FLEET
CORPORATION
PHILADELPHIA
PA.

(ABOVE)
UNITED STATES OF AMERICA *1914-1918* *76 x 51 cm*
Artist: James H. Daugherty
Issued by the Emergency Fleet Corporation in Philadelphia, this poster shows supply ships steaming to replenish Allied nations. An American eagle flies above

(RIGHT)
UNITED STATES OF AMERICA *1914-1918* *106 x 72 cm*
Artist: Kenyon Cox
A woman depicted in the heroic style stands holding an upraised sword as ships sail off to war

PAINTED BY KENYON COX, N.A.

"THE SWORD IS DRAWN THE NAVY UPHOLDS IT!"

U.S. NAVY RECRUITING STATION

115 Flatbush Avenue
Brooklyn

FIGHT OR BUY BONDS

THIRD LIBERTY LOAN

(ABOVE)
UNITED STATES OF AMERICA   *1914-1918   76 x 50 cm*
Artist: Howard Chandler Christy
A young girl carrying the American flag leads the troops on to victory

(RIGHT)
UNITED STATES OF AMERICA   *1914-1918   71 x 52 cm*
Artist: Adolph Treidler
A German soldier stand ominously with his victim at his feet, and a devastated town in the distance. The blood-soaked dagger is prominently shown

HELP
STOP
THIS

W.S.S.

BUY W.S.S.

& KEEP HIM OUT of AMERICA
NATIONAL WAR SAVINGS COMMITTEE
CONTRIBUTED by L. E. WATERMAN COMPANY

THE W F POWERS CO. LITH

5629

Come On!

buy more

LIBERTY BONDS

(RIGHT)
UNITED STATES OF AMERICA   1914-1918   76 x 51 cm
Artist: Walter Whitehead
A determined young American soldier steps over a dead German
soldier. Poster issued in Philadelphia

(ABOVE)
UNITED STATES OF AMERICA   1914-1918   76 x 50 cm
Artist: Raleigh
An American soldier steps in to prevent a German soldier from harming
a woman and child

We
need
you

(ABOVE)
UNITED STATES OF AMERICA   1914-1918
Artist: Albert Sterner
An emotive American poster featuring a Red Cross nurse with her arm
around a lady's shoulders. In a dramatic appeal for support, she points
to a wounded soldier being cared for by another member of the Red
Cross

(RIGHT)
UNITED STATES OF AMERICA   1914-1918   96 x 71 cm
Artist unknown
The way to a man's heart . . . A happy soldier munches a doughnut
while the happy doner — a Salvation Army 'lassie' — looks on

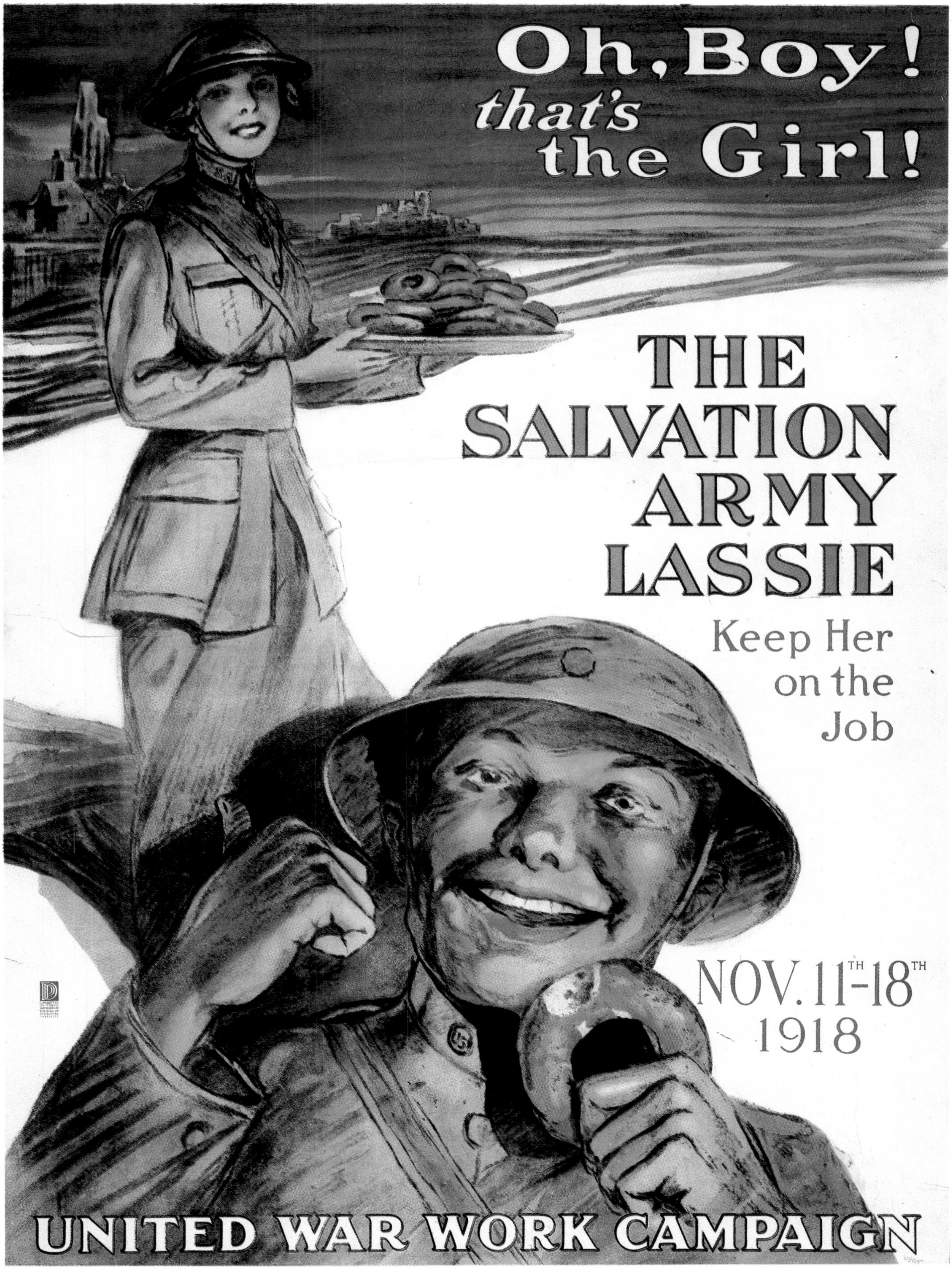
Oh, Boy!
that's
the Girl!
THE
SALVATION
ARMY
LASSIE
Keep Her
on the
Job
NOV. 11TH-18TH
1918
UNITED WAR WORK CAMPAIGN

CANADA   *1914-1918   92 x 61 cm*
Artist unknown
*A Canadian war poster featuring a picture of the Prince of Wales and
his flag. An interesting early example of the use of photographs in poster
design*

UNITED STATES OF AMERICA   *1914-1918   76 x 51 cm*
Artist: James Montgomery Flagg
Uncle Sam threatens tardy War Savings subscribers

(PAGE 66)
UNITED STATES OF AMERICA   1914-1918   84 x 56 cm
Artist: James Montgomery Flagg
*The goddess Victory, dressed in an American flag, sows the seeds of
hope upon a ploughed field. Poster issued by the National War Garden
Commission*

(PAGE 67)
UNITED STATES OF AMERICA   1914-1918   77 x 51 cm
Artist: C. R. Macaulay
*A very stern Statue of Liberty, torch in hand, pointing the finger at the
citizen down below*

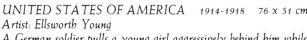

REMEMBER ·BELGIUM·

Buy Bonds
Fourth
Liberty
Loan

UNITED STATES OF AMERICA   1914-1918   76 x 51 cm
Artist: Ellsworth Young
A German soldier pulls a young girl aggressively behind him while
buildings burn in the distance. This poster capitalises on the dramatic
graphic effect of silhouette

WRITE TO THE
NATIONAL
WAR GARDEN
COMMISSION ~
WASHINGTON, D.C.
for free books on
gardening, canning
& drying.

© 1918- NATIONAL WAR GARDEN COMMISSION

JAMES MONTGOMERY FLAGG

"Every Garden a Munition Plant"

Charles Lathrop Pack, President

GERMANY   *1914-1918   76 x 50 cm*
Artist unknown
A war poster featuring a peasant farming scene. The poster says: 'Do
you want this? . . . Defend our land.'

GERMANY   1914-1918   71 x 47 cm
Artist: Paul Neumann
A German soldier holds his sword ready to strike. The poster proclaims
that 'the last strike is the eighth War Loan'

(LEFT)
CANADA   *1914-1918   89 x 61 cm*
Artists: the Brown brothers
Three French women toil in the fields. A patriotic call for French Canadians to help in the war effort

(ABOVE)
PHILIPPINES   *1914-1918   76 x 50 cm*
Artist: F Amorsota
A bilingual poster depicting an American marine being crucified and clubbed with a stone axe by the German foe

FRANCE   *1914-1918*   *110 x 78 cm*
Artist: Poulbot.
*Two young children are shown carrying a parcel and letter which
will be forwarded to their father at the Front. The caption reads 'With
this, Papa will not get a cold'.*

FRANCE   *1914-1918*   *79 x 59 cm*
Artist: Jacques Carlu
*Angry babies march with placards, demanding their rights. An
emotive poster issued by the American National Red Cross in Paris*

(PAGE 74)
FRANCE   *1914-1918*   *119 x 78 cm*
Artist: Jules Abel Faivre
*A soldier and rifle are shown. The poster calls for subscriptions to the
Second National Defence Loan and reads ' We shall get them!'*

(PAGE 75)
SOUTH AFRICA   *1914-1918*   *98 x 61 cm*
Artist: A. Holland
*Produced by the Government Printing Works in Pretoria this
recruiting poster depicts a soldier confronting a fallen German*

Der ist Schuld,

Wenn Ihr noch kämpfen
und bluten müßt
Wenn Ihr noch entbehren
müßt
Wenn Ihr Kohle und Licht
sparen müßt
Wenn Ihr Lebensmittelkarten
und Bezugsscheine braucht
Wenn Ihr Eurer friedlichen
Arbeit noch nicht nachge-
hen könnt!

Der Hauptfeind ist

England!

Darum
Bleibt einig!
Bleibt stark!
Damit verbürgt Ihr
Deutschlands
Sieg!

Klischees und Druck von Dr. Selle & Co., G. m. b. H., Berlin SW 29

GERMANY   *1914-1918   76 x 50 cm*
Artist: Leonard
*An Englishman and his bulldog . . . The poster states that 'when
Germans have to fight and bleed it is England's fault'*

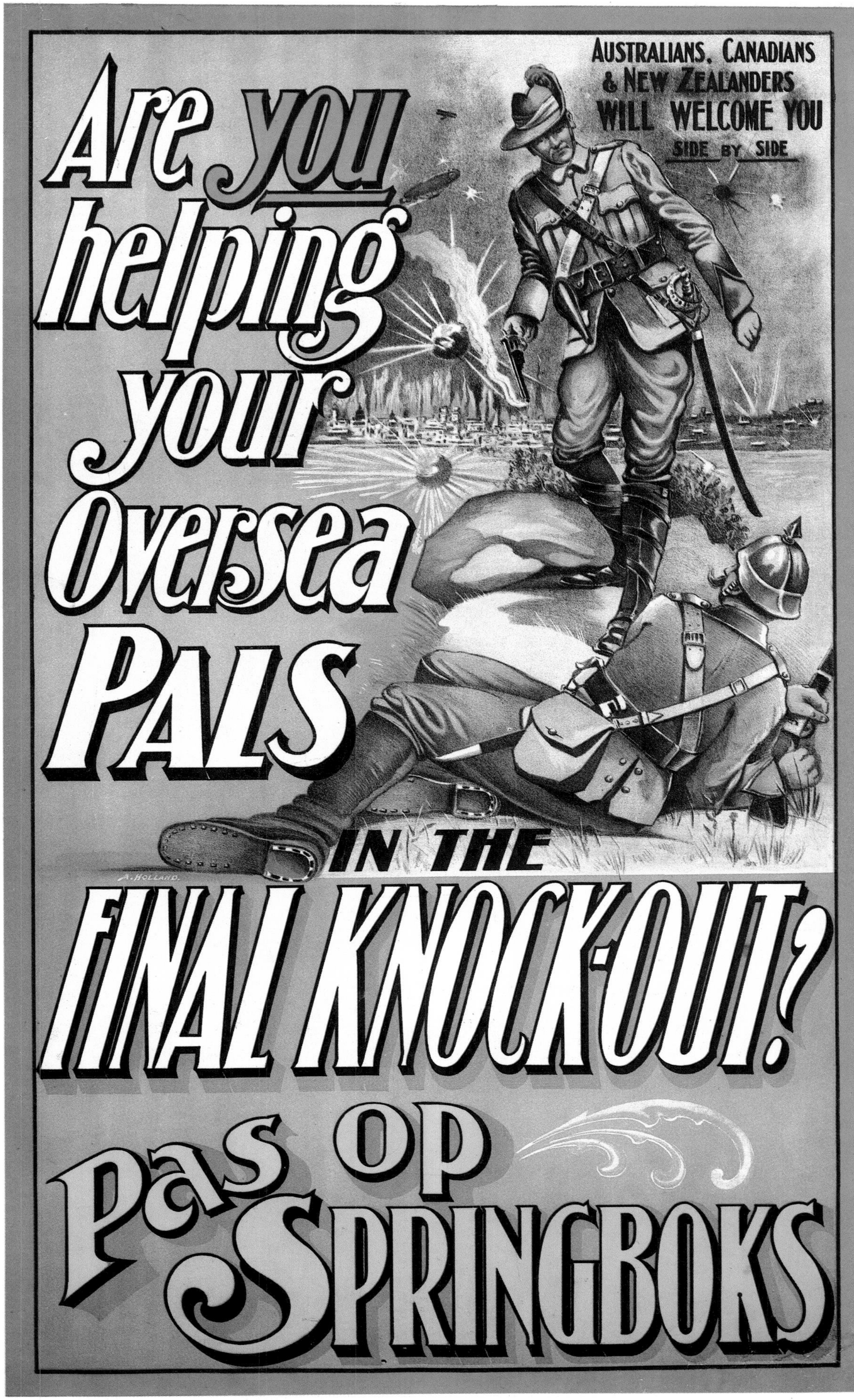
AUSTRALIANS, CANADIANS
& NEW ZEALANDERS
WILL WELCOME YOU
SIDE BY SIDE
Are you helping your Oversea PALS
IN THE
FINAL KNOCK-OUT?
Pas op SPRINGBOKS
A. HOLLAND.

FRANCE   1914-1918   114 x 76 cm
Artist: Adolphe Willette
Wife and soldier-husband embrace. The caption reads 'By ourselves at last!' The occasion is Soldiers Day — 25 and 26 December 1915

FRANCE   1914-1918   119 x 78 cm
Artist: Poulbot
A little girl plays with her wounded soldier doll, while her dog begs at her side. The poster asks people to give money on Paris Day

FRANCE *1914-1918   119 x 78 cm*
Artist unknown
Depicts injured soldiers being attended at the Western Front by Red
Cross workers. The poster asks people to buy stamps to help the Red
Cross cause

SUBSCRIBE
to the
VICTORY LOAN

Contributed by McGRATH-SHERRILL PRESS, Boston

UNITED STATES OF AMERICA   *1919   76 x 50 cm*
Artist unknown
A Yale University Press poster featuring a sketch of a bi-plane
performing aerobatic stunts. Prepared for an air show in Boston,
9 May, 1919

(RIGHT)
FRANCE   *1920   104 x 75 cm*
Artist: Louis Raemaekers
A post — World War One poster, issued in Paris, appealing for thrift.
A woman nurses six babies in a single apron. The poster proclaims a
6% saving for subscribers

l'EMPRUNT NATIONAL 6%
1920 - PRODUIT -

Louis Raemaekers.

JORDAAN & Cie
3 et 5 RUE St GEORGES 9e Arrt

Impie ALIBAUD & SALADE, 7, Rue de la Boule Rouge, PARIS_10·20.

Bolschewismus heisst

die Welt im Blut ersäufen.

Vereinigung zur Bekämpfung des Bolschewismus
Berlin W 9, Schellingstr. 2 - Fernruf: Kurfürst 5173

GERMANY   *1917-1921   32 x 24 cm*
Artist: Safis
A Russian wolf glares at a person reaching out from a pool of blood.
The caption reads: 'Bolshevism means a world of bloodsuckers'

(PAGE 82)
GREAT BRITAIN   *1939-1945   51 x 34 cm*
Artist unknown
A poster aimed at women, and emphasising the need for security
measures. A lady is shown having tea in a cafe, and discussing a
photograph of a sailor with a friend. An obviously suspect onlooker is
also listening to the conversation . . .

(PAGE 83)
GREAT BRITAIN   *1939-1945   58 x 38 cm*
Artist unknown
Three servicemen drinking and smoking with a lady who could be a
spy . . . an appeal for awareness of security measures

GERMANY   1917-1921   119 x 78 cm
Artist unknown
A German anti-Bolshevik poster depicting a heroic figure pointing to a
menacing cloud with a skull in the middle. The caption reads: 'Nations
of Europe, join in the defence of your faith and your home!'

Keep mum
she's not so dumb!

CARELESS TALK COSTS LIVES

GREAT BRITAIN   1939-1945   76 x 51 cm
Artist: Alfred Sindall
Keeping the troops warm . . . A soldier smiles as he unfolds a blanket

GREAT BRITAIN   1939-1945   76 x 51 cm
Artist unknown
The notorious 'red poster' issued early in the 1939-1945 war, which
caused much cynical comment among the British public

(PAGE 86)
GREAT BRITAIN   1939-1945   76 x 51 cm
Artist unknown
A Royal Air Force poster depicting Stirling bombers raiding the Baltic
port of Lübeck in 1942

(PAGE 87)
GREAT BRITAIN   1939-1945   50 x 37 cm
Artist: Noke
Focusing on the need for strict security measures, this poster shows a
man in two-fold dress: one half is civilian, the other in German army
officer uniform

"We kneel only to Thee"

GREAT BRITAIN   1939-1945   51 x 38 cm
Artist: Clive Uptton
A British soldier at prayer. Issued by His Majesty's Stationery Office

Heavy "Stirling" bombers raid the Nazi Baltic port of Lübeck and leave the docks ablaze

BACK THEM UP!

PRINTED FOR H.M. STATIONERY OFFICE BY FOSH & CROSS LTD., LONDON   (51-2438)

CARELESS TALK
COSTS LIVES

GREAT BRITAIN   *1939-1945   21 x 32 cm*
Artist: Fougasse
A man and woman converse over a meal while Adolf Hitler lies under
the table taking notes. This poster is notable for its use of caricature

GREAT BRITAIN   *1939-1945   38 x 26 cm*
Artist unknown
A poster from Her Majesty's Stationery Office depicting a man's foot
pushing a spade into the soil, as children smile in the background

(PAGE 90)
GREAT BRITAIN   *1939-1945   82 x 55 cm*
Artist unknown
A British war poster featuring a bus conductress at work and
incorporating a poem by A. P. Herbert

(PAGE 91)
SOVIET UNION   *1939-1945   40 x 28 cm*
Artist: A. Prokofiev
Depicts a Russian soldier killing a German who is standing on a
peasant woman. The caption reads: 'Over the land of the Soviets

GREAT BRITAIN   *1939-1945   76 x 51 cm*
Artist unknown
The allied air offensive against Germany. The map features an inset
enlargement of the Ruhr

SEEING IT THROUGH

How proud upon your quarterdeck you stand,
  Conductor—Captain—of the mighty bus!
Like some Columbus you survey the Strand,
  A calm newcomer in a sea of fuss.

You may be tired—how cheerfully you clip,
  Clip in the dark, with one eye on the street—
Two decks—one pair of legs—a rolling ship—
  Much on your mind—and fat men on your feet!

The sirens blow, and death is in the air:
  Still at her post the trusty Captain stands,
And counts her change, and scampers up the st
  As brave a sailor as the King commands.

A. P. Her

ОКНО ТАСС № 534

За страну советскую
Бей зверье немецкое.
Бей штыком, гранатой бей,
Бей, чем хочешь, но убей!

А. ПРОКОФЬЕВ.

ОГИЗ. Куйбышевское издательство. Тираж 20000. ½ п. л. Подписано к печати 28/Х 1942 г. ЕО30776. Литография «Свободный Труд» Заказ № 304. Цена 1 р. 50 к.

Художественный фонд Союза ССР.

GREAT BRITAIN   1939-1945   50 x 37 cm
Artist unknown
An appeal for thrift, aimed at the women of Britain and issued by the
National Savings Committee. We see the 'squander bug' encouraging a
woman as she shops

Coughs and sneezes spread diseases

Trap the germs by using your handkerchief

Help to keep the Nation Fighting Fit

GREAT BRITAIN   1939-1945   76 x 50 cm
Artist: H. M. Bateman
A humorous depiction of a serious problem — the spread of infectious
disease. A plea for preventive health measures, issued by the Ministry of
Health

(PAGE 94)
EGYPT   1939-1945   76 x 50 cm
Artist unknown
A cartoon caricature poster depicting Hitler and Mussolini looking at a
woman tied to a tree. The Arabic script translates as 'You are now in
my protection and nobody could deprive you of your freedom'

(PAGE 95)
MALAYA   1939-1945   38 x 27 cm
Artist unknown
A Malayan sailor takes guard, a bayonetted rifle in his hand.
A warship cruises on full alert in the distance

GREAT BRITAIN   1939-1945   76 x 50 cm
Artist: Clive Uptton
A recruitment poster, issued by the Ministry of Supply in London,
enlisting support against the Japanese

94

هتلر: انت الآن في حمايتي ولن يستطيع احد ان يحرمك حريتك!

Malaya's own navy
تنترا لأوت تانه ملايو سنديري
منولوڠ
مڠاول
تانه ملايو
A.P.B. LTD

GREAT BRITAIN   1939-1945   63 x 51 cm
Artist: Zero
Precautions for all to heed at night, and especially during blackouts

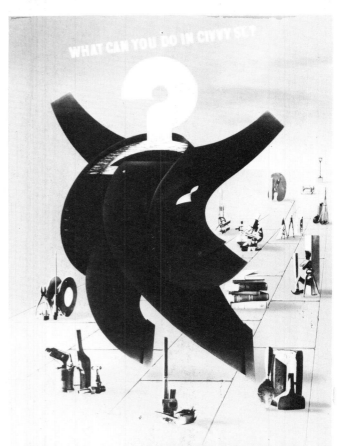

GREAT BRITAIN   1939-1945   76 x 50 cm
Artist unknown
A British war poster depicting a question mark wearing a suit. Issued by Her Majesty's Stationery Office on behalf of the Army Education programme, and highlighting career opportunities after the war

(PAGE 98)
UNITED STATES OF AMERICA   1939-1945   99 x 66 cm
Artist unknown
A poster in the caricature style depicting Hitler and Tojo caged in the flags of the allied nations

(PAGE 99)
UNITED STATES OF AMERICA   1939-1945   53 x 43 cm
Artist unknown
A particularly forceful American poster depicting a Japanese soldier in the Philippines killing an American prisoner-of-war with the butt of his rifle

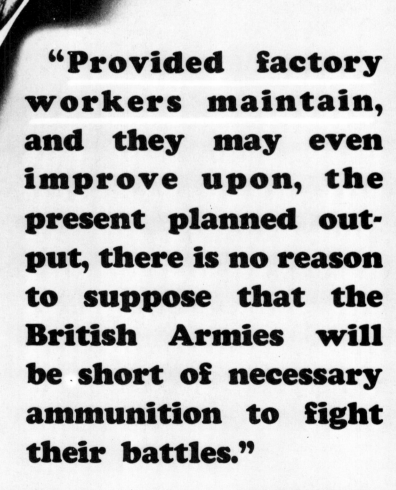

"Provided factory workers maintain, and they may even improve upon, the present planned output, there is no reason to suppose that the British Armies will be short of necessary ammunition to fight their battles."

The Prime Minister,
House of Commons,
November 28, 1944

GREAT BRITAIN   1939-1945   75 x 49 cm
Photographer unknown
A famous photograph of the British wartime leader, Sir Winston
Churchill, accompanied by extracts from his speech in the House of
Commons on 28 November 1944

What are *YOU* going to do about it?

5200 Yank Prisoners Killed by Jap Torture In Philippines; Cruel 'March of Death' Described

Soviets Near | Heavy Action Rises in Fury Crack Unit | *RAF Hurls New Blows* | Other Thousands of Victims Were Filipinos; Captives Were Starved, Beaten, Bayoneted, Shot and Even Beheaded, Army and Navy Report

STAY ON THE JOB UNTIL EVERY MURDERING JAP IS WIPED OUT!

U. S. ARMY OFFICIAL POSTER

CEYLON   *1939-1945   55 x 45 cm*
Artist unknown
*Using caricature to impress a sense of security awareness ... We are
shown a devil preying on a peasant*

A TOUS LES FRANÇAIS

La France a perdu une bataille!
Mais la France n'a pas perdu la guerre!

Des gouvernants de rencontre ont pu
capituler, cédant à la panique, oubliant
l'honneur, livrant le pays à la servitude.
Cependant, rien n'est perdu!

Rien n'est perdu, parce que cette guerre est
une guerre mondiale. Dans l'univers libre,
des forces immenses n'ont pas encore donné.
Un jour, ces forces écraseront l'ennemi. Il faut
que la France, ce jour-là, soit présente à la
victoire. Alors, elle retrouvera sa liberté et sa
grandeur. Tel est mon but, mon seul but!

Voila pourquoi je convie tous les Francais,
où qu'ils se trouvent, à s'unir à moi dans
l'action, dans le sacrifice et dans l'espérance.

Notre patrie est en peril de mort.
Luttons tous pour la sauver!

VIVE LA FRANCE !

GÉNÉRAL DE GAULLE

QUARTIER-GÉNÉRAL,
4, CARLTON GARDENS,
LONDON, S.W.1.

FRANCE   *1939-1945   75 x 50 cm*
Artist unknown
*A poster directed at French civilian and resistance groups: 'To all
Frenchmen ... Long live France! De Gaulle proclaims, "I ask all
Frenchmen, wherever they may be, to unite with me in action, in
sacrifice and in hope."'*

(PAGE 102)
UNITED STATES OF AMERICA   *1939-1945   58 x 42 cm*
Artist: Bernard Perlin
*A reference to the savage Japanese attack on Pearl Harbor in 1941.
The poster depicts an American sailor with upraised fist*

(PAGE 103)
UNITED STATES OF AMERICA   *1939-1945   102 x 73 cm*
Artist: John Falter
*A civil rights emphasis from the U.S. Government Printing Office. The
poster depicts a minister of religion and a family in the shadow of a
whip-lashing German*

GERMANY   *1939-1945   58 x 42 cm*
Artist unknown
Depicts a skeleton on a British aeroplane saying 'The enemy sees your
light! Blackout!'

"THIS WORLD CANNOT EXIST HALF SLAVE AND HALF FREE"

SACRIFICE FOR FREEDOM!

For additional copies write to Graphics Division, Office of Facts and Figures, Washington, D. C. . . . . Specify GPO Jacket No. 453126.

UNITED STATES OF AMERICA   1939-1945   51 x 36 cm
Artist: B. Arias
An uncaptioned cartoon depicting Uncle Sam and a Mexican
laughing as Hitler parachutes onto a cactus. Ridiculing the opposition
was obviously good for morale

UNITED STATES OF AMERICA   1939-1945   71 x 51 cm
Artist: I. Bingham
An American soldier casts a stern glance at the islands of Japan below.
Poster issued by the U.S. Treasury

OURS...to fight for

Freedom of Speech

Freedom of Worship

Freedom from Want

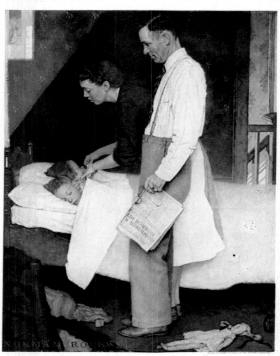

Freedom from Fear

(ABOVE)
UNITED STATES OF AMERICA   *1939-1945   58 x 41 cm*
Artist: Norman Rockwell
Emphasises the qualities of Western democracy and shows four small pictures of family life

(RIGHT)
UNITED STATES OF AMERICA   *1939-1945   73 x 51 cm*
Artist: Norman Rockwell
The family and neighbours welcome a returned soldier. Poster taken from a cover painting for Saturday Evening Post

UNITED STATES OF AMERICA   1939-1945   69 x 53 cm
Artist unknown
An appeal to end black market trade, issued by the U.S. Government
Printing Office in 1943. A black marketeer is shown being pressed
under a ration stamp by a huge thumb

UNITED STATES OF AMERICA   1939-1945   71 x 51 cm
Photographer unknown
A strong anti-Nazi statement based on the threat to democratic freedom.
We are shown Nazis burning books

(PAGE 110)
AUSTRALIA   1939-1945   57 x 39 cm
Artist: I. Northfield
A recruitment poster showing a woman in uniform, and her colleagues
working in a R.A.A.F. setting in the background. Issued on behalf of
the Women's Auxiliary Australian Air Force

(PAGE 111)
AUSTRALIA   1939-1945   76 x 51 cm
Artist: I. Northfield
Depicts a mother, her small son and their belongings and two wounded
soldiers bathing in the warm light of an angelic Red Cross nurse

UNITED STATES OF AMERICA   1939-1945   101 x 72 cm
Artist unknown
Issued in 1942 by the Division of Information in Washington, this
poster depicts a caricature of 'the German foe'

...*because somebody talked!*

UNITED STATES OF AMERICA   1939-1945   60 x 50 cm
Artist: Wesley
A melancholy spaniel on his dead master's chair — a war poster urging
care with conversation for purposes of security. Issued by the U.S.
Office of War Information, Washington

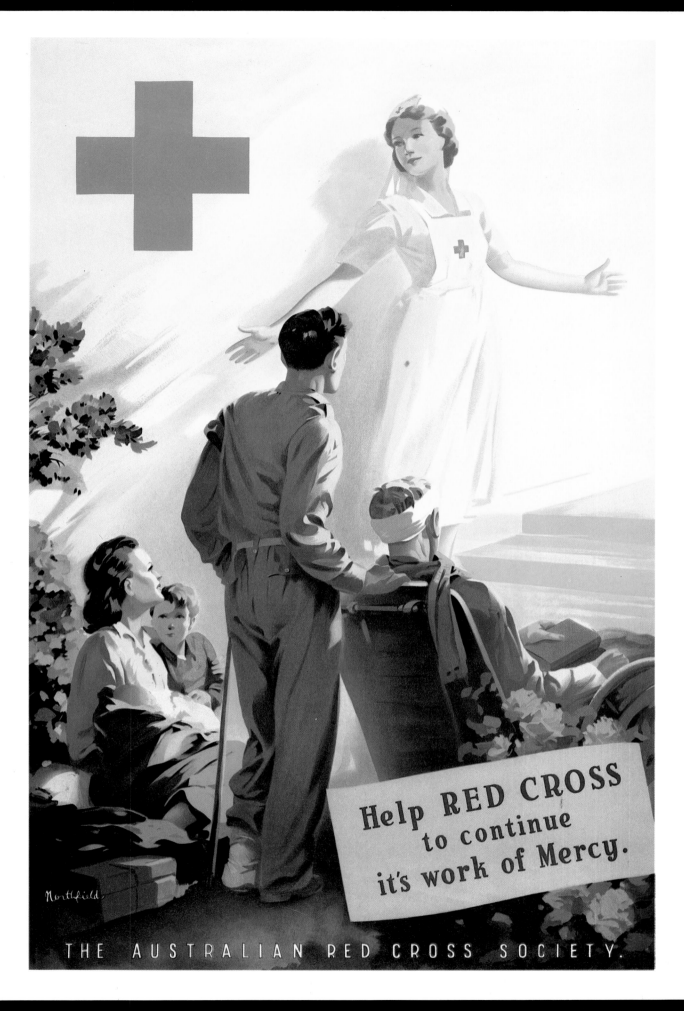

JOIN US *in a* VICTORY JOB

APPLY AT YOUR NEAREST NATIONAL SERVICE OFFICE

AUSTRALIA   1939-1945   60 x 49 cm
Artist unknown
An enlistment and recruiting poster showing women of the armed forces,
a nurse and a factory worker

AUSTRALIA   1939-1945   24 x 21 cm
Artist unknown
Australian and an American soldier are shown combining to squash
the enemy — Hideki Tojo

AUSTRALIA 1939-1945 51 x 38 cm
Artist: Norman Lindsay
*A working man pushes his sleeves up and gets ready for action. Reprint
of a painting and poem from* The Bulletin

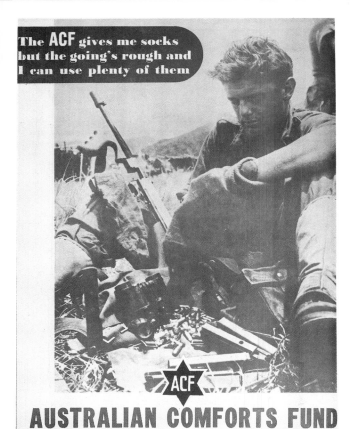

AUSTRALIA   1939-1945   50 x 37 cm
Artist unknown
Issued by the Australian Comforts Fund, this poster depicts a soldier in
New Guinea, mending his socks

AUSTRALIA   1939-1945   76 x 51 cm
Photographer unknown
An Australian poster issued before the obsolete Wirraway was
outclassed by the Japanese Zero fighter in air combat

(LEFT)
AUSTRALIA   1939-1945   39 x 26 cm
Artist unknown
A lesson in tactics and camouflage, issued by the Department of Home
Security, Canberra. One of a series of 'Apt Epitaphs'

AUSTRALIA *1939-1945   74 X 48 CM*
Artist: Walter Jardine
The technology behind warfare: valves for defence whether for use on
land, sea or air.

AUSTRALIA *1939-1945 38 x 25 cm*
Artist: Trompf
Blackout precautions on the road. An appeal to cyclists issued by the
National Safety Council of Australia

AUSTRALIA *1939-1945 38 x 25 cm*
Artist: Trompf
Issued by the National Safety Council of Australia, an appeal for
precautions during blackouts and at night

(RIGHT)
AUSTRALIA *1939-1945 44 x 30 cm*
Artist: Armstrong
The soldier as a resource — a firm reminder on how to assist the war
effort. Issued by the Australian Army

THOSE WHO TALK DON'T KNOW

THOSE WHO KNOW DON'T TALK!

ISSUED BY H.Q. VIC. L. OF C. AREA

AUSTRALIA   1939-1945   51 x 39 cm
Artist unknown
The familiar symbolism of the 'stupid galah' who talked about military
information, and the 'wise owl' who maintained silence. A Victorian poster
reproduced by an army cartographic company

AUSTRALIA   1939-1945   24 x 18 cm
Artist unknown
Conservation of vital resources during wartime. Poster issued by the
Commonwealth Coal Commission in 1944

AUSTRALIA   1939-1945   61 x 49 cm
Artist: Ian McCowan
A soldier is given his papers by a woman who has joined the
Australian Women's Army Service

(RIGHT)
AUSTRALIA   1939-1945   76 x 50 cm
Artist unknown
This Australian industry poster was issued by General Motors Holden
Pty. Limited in 1942 and posed the 'Japanese inspector' as the
adversary: 'If our work is not good enough someone will be let down
badly!'

AUSTRALIA   1939-1945   73 X 48 cm
Artist unknown
Emphasis on the Commonwealth of Nations. Australia as the food
arsenal of the allied world, sharing its produce with other
Commonwealth countries

AUSTRALIA   1939-1945   74 x 50 cm
Artist unknown
A poster urging the house-wife to save food and restrict its use. To make this point, we see her using tins of food to attack a Japanese soldier

AUSTRALIA   1939-1945   75 x 49 cm
Artist unknown
The obsequious Japanese compared with courageous, thoughtful Australians. Tojo looks particularly grim. Meanwhile coalminers toil resourcefully underground

(RIGHT)
AUSTRALIA   1939-1945   26 x 22 cm
Artist unknown
An airman converses unwittingly with one of Tojo's 'puppets' — dressed in civilian clothes. An appeal for awareness of security precautions

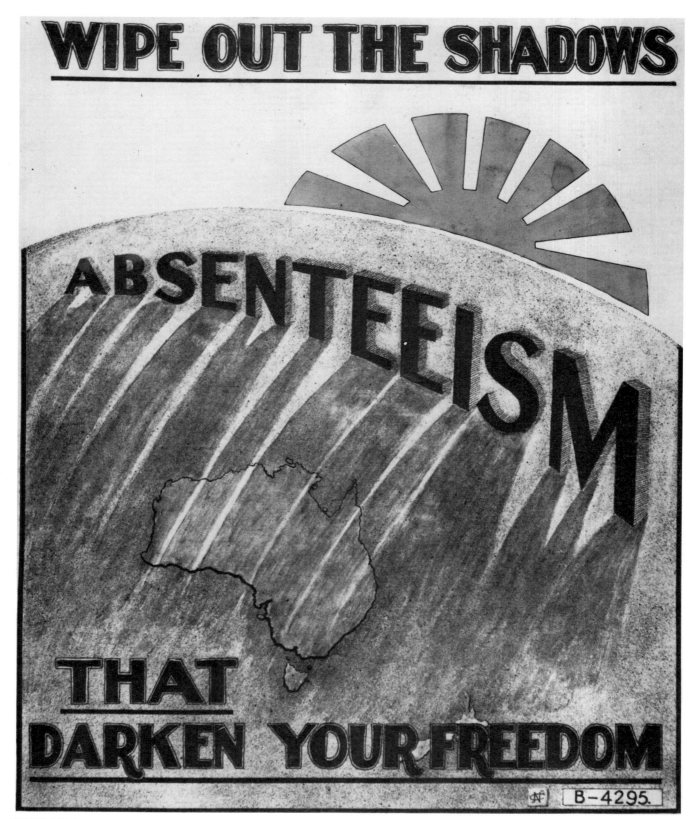

WIPE OUT THE SHADOWS

ABSENTEEISM

THAT DARKEN YOUR FREEDOM

B-4295.

AUSTRALIA   *1939-1945   50 x 40 cm*
Artist unknown
A curious mixture of symbolism: the Japanese rising sun in conjunction
with absenteeism, casts shadows across Australia

БИЛИ МЫ ВРАГА КОПЬЕМ,
WE SMASHED THE ENEMY WITH LANCES

БИЛИ МЫ ВРАГА РУЖЬЕМ,
WE SMASHED THE ENEMY WITH RIFLES

И ТЕПЕРЬ СТАЛЬНЫМ ОРУЖЬЕМ
БЬЕМ ВРАГА, ГДЕ ОБНАРУЖИМ!
AND NOW WE'RE SMASHING HIM . . . WHEREVER WE CATCH HIM

SOVIET UNION   1939-1945   76 x 51 cm
Artist: Kukryniksy
Soviet posters often depicted historic triumphs in the defence of Russia.
This example seems to refer to the defeat of the Teutonic knights in the
Middle Ages and to Russian victories in the First World War

КРАСНАЯ АРМИЯ
НЕСЕТ ОСВОБОЖДЕНИЕ
ОТ ФАШИСТСКОГО ИГА!

SOVIET UNION   1939-1945   58 x 41 cm
Artist unknown
The caption reads: 'Red Army brings liberation from the Fascist yoke'.

(RIGHT)
SOVIET UNION   1939-1945   76 x 51 cm
Artist: I. Rabichev
The determination of the Russian people to defend their homeland in the
Great Patriotic War, is evident from this poster of 1941

THE ENEMY SHALL NEVER ESCAPE OUR WRATH

They keep Australia strong

AUSTRALIA   *1950-1953   51 x 63 cm*
Artist unknown
This poster was displayed in Australia during the Korean War to promote the popular image of the fighting services

UNITED STATES OF AMERICA   *1950-1953   32 x 48 cm*
Artist unknown
A poster reproduced by the U.S. Army to alert troops in the Korean War campaign to the possibility of a resumption of hostilities should peace negotiations break down

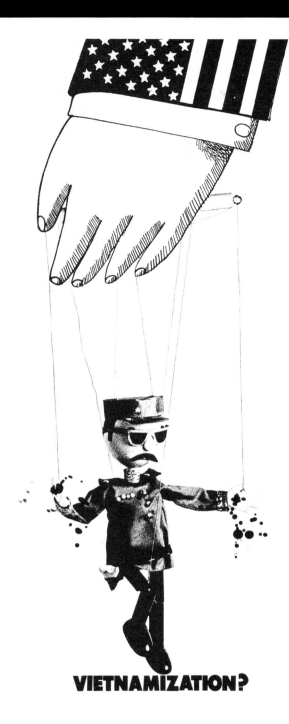

VIETNAMIZATION?

STOP THE WAR!
WITHDRAW SUPPORT FOR SAIGON REGIME
BRING TROOPS HOME
VIETNAM MORATORIUM SEPTEMBER 18

Authorised by K.J. McLeod, Sec-Convenor, Vietnam Moratorium Campaign, 232 Castlereagh St, Sydney. Tel. 26 2355   Printed by Comment Publishing Company, 22 Steam Mill Street, Sydney.

AUSTRALIA   *1961-1975*   *51 x 38 cm*
Artist unknown
Issued during the Vietnam Moratorium Campaign, this poster shows
the Vietnamese Marshal Ky as a puppet of the United States

FOUR OUT OF FIVE
OF THESE MEN
CHOSE THEIR CAREERS

ABOLISH CONSCRIPTION NOW
VIETNAM MORATORIUM SEPTEMBER 18

AUSTRALIA   1961-1975   51 x 38 cm
Artist unknown
A protest poster issued by the Vietnam Moratorium Campaign in Sydney appealing for an end to conscription. Of the five men, only the soldier is unable to choose his career

The
Silent
Majority
Made Him
Possible

YOUR
SILENCE
Made This
Possible . . . .

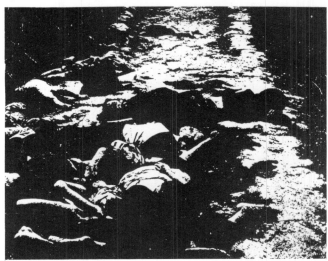

NEW ZEALAND   1961-1975   58 x 40 cm
Photographer unknown
A graphic protest poster showing portraits of Adolf Hitler and Richard Nixon above a photograph of a death scene in Vietnam

AUSTRALIA   1961-1975
Artist unknown
An Australian protest poster from the period of the Vietnamese War. A
youth shields his face from the sight of a skull: war is depicted as being
only skin-deep, a futile exercise with grim consequences

ACKNOWLEDGEMENTS

Thanks to Michael McKernan, Michael Piggot, Margaret Browne, Ena John and the staff of the Australian War Memorial for their assistance in the production of this book.

AUSTRALIAN WAR MEMORIAL REFERENCE NUMBERS

Cover: V1122; 20: V38,V1122; 21: V20; 22: V147; 23: V1155; 24: V151,149; 25: V33; 26: V5167; 27: V5005; 28: V1149, V1316, V154; 29; V39; 30: V21; 31: V148; 32: V141; 33: V26; 34: V1074; 35: V5632; 36: V19; 37: V41; 38: V7335; 39: V79; 40: V980,V1018; 41: V3933; 42: V1304; 43: V957; 44: V1305, V384; 45: V93; 46: V5305; 47: V4894; 48: V1076; 49: V1139; 50: V977; 51: V122; 52: V5621; 53: V852; 54: V1190; 55: V1195; 56: V5652; 57: V609; 58: V1; 59: V5629; 60: V5643; 61: V243; 62: V1070; 63: V805; 64: V471, V5626; 65: V1158; 66: V5642; 67: V5631; 68: V123; 69: V5962; 70: V468; 71: V111; 72: V85, V5950; 73: V27; 74: V46; 75: V97; 76: V63, V90; 77: V71; 78: V3; 79: V615; 80: V130; 81: V132; 82: V1097; 83: V362; 84: V1433, RH illustration not yet catalogued; 85: V235; 86: V2297; 87: V2631; 88: V2905, V2411; 89: V1406; 90: V249; 91: V229; 92: V1093, V1955; 93: V49; 94: V220; 95: V3252; 96: V2371, V285; 97: V1797; 98: V743; 99: V2846; 100: V290, V1616; 101: V356; 102: V350; 103: V770; 104: V190; 105: V2809; 106: V354; 107: V715; 108: V652, V2812, V1329; 109: V47; 110: V1101; 111: V193; 112: V332, V2357; 113: V2657; 114: V2847, V4271, V1106; 115: V2859; 116: V3273, V3272, V2492; 117: V2497; 118: V2338, V1048, V173; 119: V2123; 120: V46, V2176, V809; 121: V157; 122: V349, V1342; 123: V1322; 124: V211, lower illustration not yet catalogued; 125: V895; 126: V866, V318; 127: V313

JUN '86

DATE DUE			
2/28/92 RO			